Through the Storm

Roffie Ensey

Published by

Advance Ministries

For additional copies of this book, contact:
Advance Ministries
12391 Lyra Drive
Willis, TX 77318

Through the Storm
paperback edition
ISBN: 0-9706034-4-4

© 2002 Advance Ministries
All rights reserved

All scripture references are taken from the King James Version
of the Bible unless otherwise stated.

Printed in the United States by
Morris Publishing
3212 East Highway 30
Kearney, NE 68847
1-800-650-7888

Dedication

To Mother, who after eighty-four years is still taking to heart the commandment to "train up a child in the way he should go." Her children and grandchildren and great-grandchildren rise up and call her blessed. Thank you, Mother, for...

teaching me to have faith in God regardless of the circumstances

teaching me that God remains faithful even when we are not faithful

teaching me by example that it pays to serve God

being the number one teacher in my life

...all you have done to help me in my walk with God.

Special thanks to...

...my best editor, my husband. Thanks for your help with this project and for your contribution to it. You walked through this storm with me.

...my children for writing the foreword for this book. You have never acted ashamed of your mother's crooked smile and for that I am thankful.

...to my mother and sister for sharing your memories. You have always been there for me and you are both an inspiration.

...Kim Rhoads, other friends, children and grandchildren who helped with the editing. Thanks to all of you.

...Jesus, the One who kept me through this storm.

Contents

Foreword 7

Preface 11

1. Memorials 13

2. St. Louis 27

3. Diagnosis 41

4. Prayer 47

5. Surgery 53

6. Surgery Again 63

7. Home Again 69

8. Epilogue 77

9. From A Husband's Perspective 81

10. From Her Family's Perspective 89

Foreword

When Dad first tried to explain to me that it was possible that my mother might not survive the surgery she was about to have, and if she did she might be a *vegetable* for the rest of her life, I don't recall being afraid. My seven year-old mind was thinking more along the line of turnips and squash, and trying to figure out how this might happen. (My Dad patiently explained what the term "vegetable" meant in medical terms.) I think perhaps I didn't feel too fearful because I hadn't seen my mother act as if she was afraid. And if she wasn't afraid of it, I didn't suppose I should be either.

I can't think of very many things that my mother is afraid of, outside of snakes and heights. She once chopped up my rubber cobra with a butcher knife! And to this day she can hardly ride in glass elevators. But she has never been afraid to tackle anything that life has thrown her way. I have never known her to back down from a job or say she couldn't do it. And most of the time she could!

I don't remember my mother ever crying over her condition or what she had been dealt in life. Rather, I remember her finding something to laugh about in it all. I learned from her that it is a good thing to be able to laugh at yourself. You see, my mother is the lady with the crooked smile and the straight heart. She may have some paralysis in her face, but I have never seen her paralyzed by fear. She may have a deaf ear, but I have never known her to miss the voice of God. I count myself a son blessed above all others to have a mother like mine. She has been a living lesson of faith.

As you read this book, I think you will find my mother's constant trust in God shining through. Today, thirty-three years after she wasn't supposed to survive, she is still inspiring others. As her pastor, I can proudly say nobody has a more *faithful* saint. I love you, Mother!

Randy Ensey, Pastor
Living Way Church
Conroe, Texas

Since I was only about four years old at the time of the events in this book, I don't remember a lot about the specifics. The things that I remember came later. But in a way, it's not really what I do remember, but what I don't remember that counts. I don't remember ever hearing my mother complain about the way she looked, the fact that she couldn't hear in one ear, or any of the other things about which many of us may have complained. I don't remember ever hearing her use these physical signs as an excuse not to do something. My mother taught my brother and I that those things really didn't matter when placed against what God had done for her.

This story, which I heard over and over, never got old for me because every time I heard it I realized that I was once again hearing about a miracle—an Ebenezer—in our lives. "What do these stones mean, Mother?" They mean that God has done it before and He will do it again! They mean that He is faithful! They mean that I don't have to fear that He has forsaken us!

What a rich heritage to always have in front of me a mother and a father who taught, not only with their words, but with their lives that God is faithful. I have spoken to so many people over the years about my mother and what God did for her, and I have had the privilege of hearing what that testimony has meant to others. My mother is the most beautiful woman I know because her beauty comes from the inside, from the One who lives in her heart and guides her daily, and that makes her shine!

I love you, Mom!

>Debbie Black, Pastor's Wife
>First United Pentecostal Church
>Statesville, North Carolina

Preface

In the past thirty-three years I have had the privilege of sharing my testimony with thousands of people. Many of them came to me later to say they had shared the tape with a friend who was going through a similar circumstance.

My motivation for putting this in book form is for those yet to come. I want my grandchildren and my great-grandchildren to be able to read this and realize the God we serve is indeed One who can be trusted!

May the Lord strengthen and encourage all who read this.

To the peoples, nations and men of every language, who live in all the world: May you prosper greatly! It is my pleasure to tell you about the miraculous signs and wonders that the Most High God has performed for me. How great are his signs, how mighty his wonders! His kingdom is an eternal kingdom; his dominion endures from generation to generation (Daniel 4:1-3 NIV).

Roffie
age 17

Jerry & Roffie Ensey
Evangelistic Team
1960

Memorials

When the children of Israel left Egypt, they had no idea what was in store for them. God told them to go, He made a way for them to go, and they went. They had witnessed the miracles of God during the time Moses was negotiating with Pharaoh for their freedom, but they really had no conception of God's abundant supply of riches. During their forty years in the wilderness they found that He could supply water from a rock when they needed it. He could provide food—even meat when they desired it. They discovered the shoes on their feet grew with them and did not even wear out on this long trek through the wilderness.

Later Moses reminded them of how

and why God led them through the wilderness:

> *Remember how the LORD your God led you all the way in the desert these forty years, to humble you and to test you in order to know what was in your heart, whether or not you would keep his commands* (Deuteronomy 8:2 NIV).

When they came to the Jordan River to cross over into the Land of Promise, Joshua had the priests take the ark and step out into the water. The waters parted and the Israelites walked across on dry land. They didn't even get mud on their shoes. This was just another miracle from the hand of their God. After they had all crossed over, Joshua instructed twelve men to go back and each pick up a stone from the riverbed. These twelve stones were to be used to build a memorial. Later, when their children would ask what the stones meant they could tell them about the miracles God had performed for them in Egypt and on their travels through the desert.

We sometimes look at this narrative and wonder how the Israelites could forget so quickly. One day He brings water from a rock and the next day they are complaining because they miss the garlic from Egypt and think they are going to starve to death in the wilderness. How could they so easily fall back into doubting that God would take care of them?

When we think about it rationally we can conclude that it is for the same reason we let doubt and fear fill our lives. We forget to look back and consider what God has done for us in the past.

God has provided for us, He has healed our bodies, He has worked miracles for us. However, many times we fail to look back at our Ebenezers and be strengthened by them. There are memorials in all of our lives. This book tells of some of mine.

Mother received the Holy Ghost before I was born and Daddy was converted when I was just a child. So I was raised in a family that knew and loved the truths we still hold dear today—the Oneness of God, water baptism in the name of Jesus Christ, the wonderful gift of the Holy Ghost, and a Christian lifestyle that honors the Lord.

I remember times as a child when my mother told us about walking to church in the rain when she had four children under five years of age. I was one of those four and she taught me through her dedication that it is worth whatever we have to go through to live for God. She taught me by her example that you gain strength from being in God's presence. She instilled in me a love for the house of God.

Mother started from the time each of us came into this world to put the Word of God in our hearts. She continually told us Bible stories, taught us facts from the Bible, and even gave us quizzes when we were older. She taught all of us the books of the Bible at an early age. Through this she instilled a love for His Word in each of us.

When I was about seven, my only sister, Gaye, came along. It was hurricane season in Texas and one was blowing in. The wind was blowing so hard the little pine trees around our house were bending over and almost touching the earth. Before the rain came, Mother picked up Gaye and walked outside with her. Of course, my brothers and I followed. She realized we were afraid, so she walked and talked to us. I do not remember her exact words, but I still remember the message she gave us: "I know the wind is blowing and a storm is on the way. I know it looks chaotic right now, but the God we serve is in control. The Bible tells us He controls the winds and the waves!"

From that little encounter she instilled in me a trust in God. From that day forward I knew that God has His way in the storm and in the whirlwind.

The LORD hath his way in the whirlwind and in the storm, and the clouds are the dust of his feet (Nahum 1:3).

To this day I have never been afraid in a storm. On one occasion during a storm in Kansas the wind approached 100 mph, but I did not feel fear! Why? I remembered the memorial Mother put in my life.

Another memorial happened at the age of sixteen when I fully gave my heart to Jesus. I realized that God has no grandchildren. I couldn't make it on my parents' faith or experience. I had to develop my own relationship with Him. I had to have an experience with God for myself. The greatest miracle He ever did for me was when He washed away my past with His blood. He lost the record of my sins in the sea of forgetfulness when I was baptized in His name, and they will never be remembered against me again. He filled me with the precious gift of the Holy Ghost and I spoke in other tongues as the spirit gave utterance.

At the age of eighteen I married a wonderful man. God brought him into my life and for that I am eternally thankful. Jerry has been the high priest and spiritual leader in our home for the past forty-two years.

My husband and I evangelized for a few months before going to Greensboro, North Carolina, to start a home missions work. There were only two UPCI churches in the state when we went there. One church was one hundred miles away and the other was two hundred miles away. In those days there were no Christmas for Christ offerings to help home missionaries. However, my home church did pledge to send us ten dollars a week. They later increased it to twenty. That doesn't seem like much now but we were able to use that money to rent a place for services on Sunday mornings. The rest of the time we had church in our home.

While there we witnessed many miracles of divine provision which became memorials in our lives. Remembering them still strengthens us today.

When we could not afford to buy or even rent a church building, God provided one rent free! We had services in that little church for two years. During that time we were able to buy property in an excellent location and build a new brick building. We built the fifty-five hundred square foot building for $20,000. The congregation in Greensboro has added on and remodeled the church since that time, but were still in the same building in 2002. (Just recently, the property was sold for over $600,000!)

So many times during those years He met our needs before we even asked. My husband says we didn't miss any meals during that time, but we postponed a few. We have certainly made up for it since then.

One of the times He provided was when we were on our way to a fellowship meeting in Wilmington, a four-hour drive from Greensboro. We filled the car with gas on our credit card and as we were pulling out of the station we drove through the parking lot of a shopping center where there was a large grocery store. My husband noticed a package of bread rolls on the ground which had obviously fallen from someone's shopping cart. No one was around at the time so it looked like manna from heaven. He said, "I am going to pull up beside that package of rolls and you lean out and pick it up." "Why don't you pull by them on your side and you lean out and get them?" I retorted. (Isn't it amazing that even in need we still have pride?!) Of course, I was the one who had to finally pick it up! With less than fifty cents in our pocket we had thought we would not get to eat until after service that night when the host church would provide sandwiches. With these rolls, however, we were able to stop and buy a small can of Spam and one drink and we enjoyed a meal on the way! This was a memorial we still remember with special fondness.

Another memorial was the birth of a healthy baby boy. During the time I was pregnant we did not always have an abundance of food to eat. Money was very scarce. I did not have vitamins to take or even sufficient milk to drink to help supply the extra calcium needed for healthy bones. When Randy was born, however, he weighed eight pounds and eight ounces and was very healthy. He was virtually never sick as a child. Even the normal childhood diseases were very mild for him. God gave us another memorial. Although those were lean times, we all stayed healthy during those years in Greensboro and God always supplied our needs. We seemed to always have just enough to pay our basic bills.

During a particularly trying period, the Lord gave us a promise He faithfully kept. After we prayed one morning I pulled this promise out of our little promise box:

The L*ORD* *shall open unto thee his good treasure, the heaven to give the rain unto thy land in his season, and to bless all the work of thine hand:* (Deuteronomy 28:12).

We rejoiced in faith and God was true to His Word! We still marvel at the many ways He blessed us.

A few years later as we were leaving

Greensboro—pulling a 5X7 trailer loaded with all our earthly possessions—my husband said to me, "If we ever doubt God again, He would be justified in striking us dead on the spot."

Pastor Ensey and Family
Greensboro, NC

First Service in Greensboro
Gilford Community Center
Rent $10.00 per week

Rent-Free Church
Greensboro, NC

New Building
Calvary Apostolic Church
Greensboro, NC

Jerry & Roffie Ensey
Silsbee, Texas
1965

St. Louis

We returned to Texas in December of 1964. Our daughter, Debbie was born in February of 1965. Jerry had just been appointed Coordinator of the Evangelism Commission, a part of the Home Missions Division at our international headquarters office in St. Louis. This was only a part-time position, so he commuted from Silsbee, Texas to St. Louis for two years as our ministry and responsibilities gradually expanded.

In 1967 he became the General Secretary of the Home Missions Division and we moved to St. Louis to assume those responsibilities.

Then the storm came! I was twenty-seven years old, with two children—Randy, seven, and Debbie, four.

Many times we hold to the illusion that when storms come into our lives, either God must not be with us or we must not be in His will. There is a story recorded in Luke chapter eight that refutes this theory.

> *One day Jesus said to his disciples, "Let's go over to the other side of the lake." So they got into a boat and set out. As they sailed, he fell asleep. A squall came down on the lake, so that the boat was being swamped, and they were in great danger* (Luke 8:22-23 NIV).

Notice that Jesus was in the boat with them and the storm came anyway! Just because we have a storm in our life doesn't mean Jesus has left us. Sometimes He leads us in a certain path to test us, to know what is in our heart, to find out whether we will keep His commands.

If we can remember that God is in control—not us, not the doctor, not the naysayers, but God—we will be able to stand through any trial that comes our way.

Being confident of this very thing, that he which hath begun a good work in you will perform it until the day of Jesus Christ (Philippians 1:6).

Trusting in God will keep us from believing the lies of the devil when he comes around to tell us that God has forsaken us. Trust is what helped Job remember that even though he could not see God, God knew right where he was.

But if I go to the east, he is not there; if I go to the west, I do not find him. When he is at work in the north, I do not see him; when he turns to the south, I catch no glimpse of him. But he knows the way that I take; when he has tested me, I shall come forth as gold (Job 23:8-10 NIV).

Job was going through a difficult storm, but he knew without a doubt God was still in control.

My storm started with a loss of hearing. There was a severe ringing in my left ear so I went to the doctor to find out what was causing this. After checking my hearing, he informed me that I was definitely losing my hearing in the left ear and these things just happen as we get older. I was only twenty-seven years old and did not think that should be the reason for this problem. He recommended a hearing aid, which I tried and could not use. It did not help at all.

Shortly after this episode I began to have severe headaches. At first they were manageable, but quickly got to the place of being unbearable. The doctor I went to for the headaches gave me some very strong pain medicine. However, even this would not stop the pain for very long. All it did was ease the pain a little and put me to sleep for a while. After about two hours the pain would return with a vengeance and wake me from a deep sleep.

With two small children it was not easy to keep going when I felt so bad all of the time. Just getting out of bed was a major chore. Randy was in the first grade, my husband had to be at work by eight o'clock, and Debbie was still home with me.

Then my equilibrium began to go. Many times just walking across the floor, I would fall. We lived in the second-story flat of an old house in South St. Louis which was built before the turn of the century. One day someone rang the doorbell and when I started down the stairs to answer the door, I fell into a window on the landing. It was a stained glass window with metal strips, and thankfully it did not give way. If it had broken, I would have fallen to the street below (about twenty feet), probably to my death.

My hair began to be a major concern because it was breaking off and falling out. I was losing my "glory" and did not know what to do about it. I knew in my heart this was a symptom of what was causing the headaches. I mentioned this to the doctor but it was always brushed aside as not a big deal. However, I did not relish the idea of being bald!

During this time, I consulted several doctors. One of them told me, after a complete exam, that he could find nothing wrong with me. He said I was losing muscle tone and that jogging a couple of miles each day would help. I wondered how I could jog when I could not walk without stumbling. I left his office very disillusioned and disappointed with doctors in general.

By now you may be wondering why I did not just pray about the situation and call for the elders of the church to have them pray for me. All my life I had been taught about the power of prayer. When we were sick as children we were always prayed for.

So every time I was in church, I asked for special prayer. I knew God could heal me, otherwise I would not have asked for prayer. Ministers and laypeople from all over the world were praying for me, along with friends and family. I still meet people from time to time who tell me that they remember praying for me during that time. But God chose not to heal me supernaturally.

It is beyond my comprehension how when two people are prayed for in the same service, one receives healing and the other does not. I cannot explain how God works. His ways are far above our ways. But this one thing I know: I **know** God does heal! He does perform miracles. I can't explain the how and why or the when; all I know is that He is still in the miracle-working business. He still heals!

If we could figure out the formula for healing—take steps one, two, and three then God has to heal us—then *we* would be in control; *we* would be God. But God in His infinite wisdom and knowledge knows what is best in each situation, and He also knows the purpose for storms that come to each of us. He does not always miraculously heal. Children of God get sick, sometimes they suffer long, and then die. Sometimes He heals, performing a miracle right before our eyes. When we study the Bible we find that God did not always deliver:

> *Women received back their dead, raised to life again. Others were tortured and refused to be released, so that they might gain a better resurrection. Some faced jeers and flogging, while still others were chained and put in prison. They were stoned; they were sawn in two; they were put to death by the sword. They went about in sheepskins and goatskins, destitute, persecuted and ill-treated—the world was not worthy of them. They wandered in deserts and mountains, and in caves and holes in the ground. These were all commended for their faith,* **yet none of**

them received what had been promised (Hebrews 11:35-39 NIV).

At times we mistakenly lay blame where it is undeserved. So many times I remember leaving a church service feeling guilty, feeling like it was all my fault because I was not healed. We often make trite, standard statements to people going through a storm: "According to your faith, so be it." And the message comes through, "If you had enough faith, you could walk out of here a well person tonight." So when it does not happen, the person who is needing a miracle leaves with the nagging fear that somehow his faith or his walk with God is deficient.

Faith is not just a mental exercise in positive thinking. You cannot think long enough or hard enough to *make* something happen. It is not faith in our faith that is needed, but faith in God!

Faith in God says, "God, I don't understand what is happening to me, but I trust you. You know what is best for me, even though I cannot see. I rest secure in your care."

In other words, I may have cancer, but cancer doesn't have me! I belong to God and He cares for me, therefore I can trust Him. I know that He is the only one who holds the keys to life and death and I will not leave this world until He permits it.

Faith is not a weapon but a shield—to protect! The shield of faith is what helps us keep our spirit and attitude right in spite of the circumstances of life.

I felt like the three Hebrew children must have felt: I will do what He requires of me, and if He chooses to deliver me completely, fine; if not, I don't have to give an answer to anyone or try to explain the reasons why God directs my life as He does.

I began to have double vision which made it difficult to do the normal things a mother needs to do. Just going to the grocery store was a major chore. I could not walk down the aisles in the store and see what I needed with just a glance. I would have to stop and allow time for my eyes to focus on each product before I could tell what it was.

Sometimes driving at night became a problem. I would see two of every car coming toward me. An eighteen wheeler would look like an enormous bridge. That summer, after visiting with my parents in Texas, I was driving back to St. Louis with my children (my husband did not get to go). James and Jean Boatman, who lived in the flat below us, were from Texas also. We met and were driving back together when I realized I had to have help or I was going to kill all of us. I stopped and told the Boatmans what was happening. Jean drove the rest of the way for me, leaving James to manage their two children and drive also. (Thank you, James and Jean!) It was really a frightening and traumatic experience.

I wore glasses, so shortly after this driving experience I decided that perhaps my headaches were caused by needing my glasses changed. I made an appointment and went to have my eyes checked.

The optometrist looked into my eyes and said, "You don't even need glasses! However, you do have a problem that I am not qualified to handle, so I am going to check with my friend who is an ophthalmologist and have him see you."

He went into another room to call the ophthalmologist. He came back and said he had been able to make an appointment for later that very morning. In those days in St. Louis, this was unheard of. Many times you had to wait weeks just to get an appointment with a doctor, particularly if you were a new patient! (God is still in control!)

When the ophthalmologist looked into my eyes he said, "Yes, you do have a problem, but it is out of my field. You need to see a neurologist. Let me call my friend and see when he can examine you."

Just as the optometrist had done, he went into another room and called the neurologist. He was out of the country on vacation, but his nurse said he would see me his first day back in the office. Again, this was very unusual, because I was a new patient. The date would be September 2, 1969. This was the latter part of August, so I had a few days to wait.

During this time the headaches were unbearable. I would take the strongest medication the doctors could give me and the pain would subside for only about two hours. Then I would have two hours of excruciating pain before I could take anything else.

I do not know how I would have made it without the Boatmans. They went beyond the call of duty, the second mile! Jean became a dear friend (more like a sister to me) and took over my children. She just added them to her two and every day Debbie spent the day with their daughter, Melanie, while I spent most of the day in bed. This had been the pattern for some time and continued through August.

Randy, age 7
Debbie, age 4
St. Louis, MO

Diagnosis

September 2 finally came and I went to see the neurologist. After a brief examination, which included sticking sharp needles into my face, he said, "I want you to go straight to the hospital (Barnes Medical Center). I will call and make arrangements." He evidently knew something was terribly wrong.

"But I am not prepared to go to the hospital. I need to go home first," I protested.

He replied, "Your husband can go get your things, but you need to be in the hospital now!! You definitely have a problem and it requires immediate attention!"

In the hospital I was turned over to Dr. Schwartz, a neurosurgeon, who taught brain surgery at the medical college in St. Louis. My sister-in-law who lived in San Antonio at the time asked a brain surgeon there about Dr. Schwartz. He replied, "He is the best there is. He is the grandaddy of brain surgery." We felt relieved and fortunate to have someone of his knowledge and caliber to handle my case.

After several days of intense testing, X-rays, CAT scans, dye tests, and hearing tests, I was taken back to my room. My husband, who stayed by my side through it all, decided to go back to his office for a while. After he left Dr. Schwartz came to my room to tell me what he had found. I was alone when he broke the news. I am sure he did not expect the response he got from me when he said, "Roffie, we have found your problem. You have a brain tumor. It is such a shame for a young woman like you to have this."

At that time, just when I needed it, God

gave me a calm and a peace that cannot be described. The peace of God that transcends understanding flooded my soul.

Dr. Schwartz evidently expected me to fall apart, and when I didn't, he continued: "Your tumor is very large and in an extremely difficult place to get to. It is underneath the cerebellum, pressing against the brain stem, and wrapped around a nerve. It is operable. However, *if* you live through the surgery, you could be a vegetable for the rest of your life. Or you could be paralyzed, either partially or fully. There could be brain damage. At best you will have memory loss and may have to learn all the basics again—how to walk, talk, read, and so forth." (We learned later that virtually any time the brain is touched there is some damage done.)

Evidently Dr. Schwartz was not getting the response from me he expected, so he said, "Young lady, where is your husband? I need to talk with him!"

My husband had gone back to work, so I gave Dr. Schwartz his phone number. He called him to come in for consultation. I am sure Dr. Schwartz got the reaction he was looking for from my husband. It is always easier to go through something yourself than to watch someone you love go through it.

I think Dr. Schwartz thought the brain tumor must have already affected my mind. My mind had been affected by something, but it was not the tumor. It was parents who taught me that God has His way in the storm and you can trust Him!

I learned a valuable lesson that day. I learned that God does not give us strength to fight imaginary battles. We often wonder what we would do in a certain situation, even thinking through a certain scenario and living it out in our mind. But strength does not come for imagined battles. It is in the heat of the real battle that we receive strength.

Jesus said to Paul, "My strength is made perfect in weakness" (II Corinthians 12:9). Hebrews 11 speaks of those who "out of weakness were made strong." I learned that just when I needed Him, He was there to strengthen me *in* the fight!

That is just what He did. I was not totally alone that afternoon—although none of my family or friends were there at that moment—because Jesus was with me.

He promised—

I will never leave thee, nor forsake thee (Hebrews 13:5).

—and He did not fail!

Prayer

That night I had a lot of concerned visitors. They came and prayed, talked, and worried about what was going to happen. I continually reassured all of them that everything was going to be all right.

I did not do this because I was such a super-spiritual person. I could do this because God had visited me that afternoon and reassured me He was in control. I had received a strength and reassurance that would stay with me through the whole ordeal. In fact, that peace is still with me to this day. I *know* my God is in control.

I was so convinced that this was not a

big deal that when my husband came into my room and told me my mother and daddy, my sister and her husband, his brother, sister, mother and stepfather were coming, I wondered out loud why they were coming. I am sure everybody there thought I was out of my mind!

One of the things that really stands out in my mind about this night are the "Job's comforters" that came to see me. When visiting someone in the hospital who could possibly be terminal, the last thing you want to tell them is about your relative who had the same thing and is no longer with us!

After my visitors all left that night, I began to think maybe I *should* be a little upset about the situation, but I could not seem to get even a *little* worried.

Usually the nurse came around with the medication about this time, but before she came to me, I took time to pray. I prayed the simplest—and yet the most effective—prayer of my life that night.

I simply prayed, "God, I'm Your child

and You know where I am and what is wrong with me right now! Lord, if it be Your will to take me, then that's fine with me. I only ask one thing: let me be ready to meet You. I want my heart right with You. But Lord, You know that I have two small children who need their mother. My husband is working for You and he needs my help. So if You see fit to leave me here, let everything be okay."

At that moment I didn't see any apparitions, angels, or bright lights. He didn't send an angel to me; **He came**! I praised Him as Jeremiah did so long ago: "Great is Thy faithfulness, Lord, unto me!"

I didn't see anyone come into my room, but I felt the strong arms of my Savior as He wrapped me in them and said softly, "Yes, I know where you are and what's going on. And I just want to remind you that I am in control! You see, I have My way in the storm!" Underneath, I felt the everlasting arms of Jesus.

A peace that passes understanding and

a confidence enveloped me. A warm feeling flowed through me and I drifted off to sleep and slept the whole night through without any pain medication—something I had not done in months! I woke the next morning with the awareness that He had given me a memorial I could hold on to—sleep with no pain for eight hours! I woke with my heart still full of that same abiding faith in God I had felt the day before!

I did not receive my healing, but I knew without a doubt that God was with me. I knew that He had plans for my life:

> *"For I know the plans I have for you,"* declares the LORD, *"plans to prosper you and not to harm you, plans to give you hope and a future"* (Jeremiah 29:11 NIV).

That weekend they gave me a pass to go home because they thought it could be the last time for me to be with my family. Our friends came and brought food, but left us mostly to ourselves so we could savor this time together.

My brother and sister-in-law, Ron and Cheryl Oliver, had come by a few days earlier and taken Debbie to Mother. So it was just Randy and my husband and I, but we had a wonderful weekend together.

My good friend Bessie Pugh came on Saturday and washed my hair for me. She was so gentle and patient and did a wonderful job of getting my scalp squeaky clean before I had to go back to the hospital and let them shave my head. In fact, the man who shaved my head said he had never seen a scalp so clean. Thank you, Sister Pugh, for your sweet thoughtfulness during that time.

Surgery

The only thing that really brought tears to my eyes during this whole ordeal was the day they shaved my head. That is still a very painful memory because they took away my "glory," all except for a little tuft right in front.

When they came to the room to tell us they were ready to take me down to shave my head, Mother and my sister braided my hair in two braids and cut them off while we all cried. I still have those braids as a reminder.

A nurse then shaved my head as clean as a man's face. After that a doctor came in and drilled a hole in the top of my head and took out a piece of bone the size of a nickel. This was done to relieve the pressure on my brain. I was scheduled for surgery the next morning.

The day I went to surgery, the nurse who took me down cried all the way. I kept trying to tell her everything was going to be okay, but she had taken many patients to this kind of surgery before and she knew how it would be—or thought she knew. Her confidence was in the doctors. But I was not putting my confidence in man who had only studied about the brain; my confidence was in the One who made this brain. He would not fail me. He was the One in control!

They needed to do one last test before surgery to help them pinpoint exactly where the tumor was. They strapped me in a chair that looked much like an electric chair with a hole in the back where my spine was. They took ten cubic centimeters of fluid from my spine and put in ten cubic centimeters of air, then turned me upside down to allow the air to surround the tumor.

X-rays were taken to determine the exact location and size of the tumor. This took much longer than they had expected it to and was tremendously painful. I found out later the reason it took so long was that they could not believe what they were seeing. The tumor was much larger than they had originally estimated. The tumor was indeed in a delicate place, under the cerebellum, and it was the size of a very large lemon or a small pear!

From there I went to surgery. The surgery took seven and one-half hours. When it was finished the anesthesiologist began talking to me to wake me. I opened my eyes in the operating room and said, "Give me a blanket—I am cold!" They were not expecting any audible response at this point, much less a rational request.

One of the men in the operating room came to see me a few days later and told me, "We have never had anybody come out of that kind of surgery talking like you did."

When they took the tumor out, they also took the eighth nerve around which the tumor had grown, leaving the left side of my face paralyzed. I could not close my left eye, and the tear ducts could not provide moisture for that eye, leaving it very dry.

After a brief time in recovery, they put me in ICU and allowed my family to come in one at a time. I am sure it was quite a shock for them to see me like I was. My shaved head was covered with an antiseptic medicine the color of ocher and swathed in bandages. There was a clear plastic cover over my eye, attached to a rubber band that was around my head. This left eye could not be closed, so I lay there with one eye open and one eye closed.

My family had been warned that I probably would not know them and would not be able to talk. But as each one of them came in, I recognized them. I called each of them by name and talked with them.

My husband came in first and I asked him if he had called the people we promised to call after surgery. He looked at me with a little grin and said, "No, I don't have their phone numbers with me."

I said, "If you have a pen and paper, I'll give you their numbers!" And I did. (Remember, I was not expected to be able to talk or have a memory!)

On the second day in ICU, I looked around me at the thirteen patients with whom I shared this ward. We were all brain surgery patients, and I was the only one who was alert and rational. The rest of them were either in a comatose state or out of their head and just jabbering.

I was even able to sit up in bed. When they came around to check each of us, I was the only one who could answer any of their trite questions—where I was, what day of the week it was, and who was the current president of the United States. It was actually fun watching the surprised expressions on their faces.

I was able to squeeze their hands and move my feet and legs. There was no paralysis except in my face!

As I begin to think of how good God was and what He had already done for me, the tears began to flow. I say "tears," but actually it was only one tear because of the paralysis in the left side of my face. A single tear slipped down my right cheek and I began to sing softly to myself.

My bed was positioned at the nurse's station, with her desk almost at the foot of my bed. When I began to sing, she looked up over the rim of her glasses at me. You could almost read her thoughts: "We have been waiting for this and here it is. She has really gone off the deep end this time."

Here is what I sang…

Till the storm passes over
and the thunder sounds no more,
Till the clouds roll forever
from the sky,
Hold me fast, let me stand,

in the hollow of thy hand.
Keep me safe till this storm
passes by.

Later I realized that this is just what He did.

God has two ways to deal with the storms in our lives. He can calm the storm or He can keep us safe *through* the storm. He chose to keep me safe through the storm. God still has His way in the storm!

When my husband came in at the next visiting opportunity I was propped up in bed. I told him, "I sang them a song." He said, "You what?" "I sang them the song 'Till the Storm Passes By.'" We both had a good cry!

Doctors had told us that the third day after brain surgery the brain swells. When my family came in to see me that morning the chaplain met them and told them, "This is the critical day. We could lose her, so don't be surprised at what you find. You may want to stop by the chapel before you go up."

So while my family was in the chapel praying, Dr. Schwartz came in to see me in ICU. After talking with me a few minutes, he asked me if I would be willing to go to a doctors' conference in the hospital auditorium. He said they would take me down on a gurney.

He wanted the other doctors to see me because this was the result they would like to see in *all* their brain surgery patients. I agreed to go to the meeting on one condition: he had to get me out of ICU. He agreed that he would find me a room and move me out of there.

I went to the conference and talked with numerous doctors, interns, and medical students. They examined me and talked with me for about an hour, marveling at my progress. When they wheeled me back to ICU, the nurse confirmed that they had found a room for me.

Of course I was ready to go right then, so I asked what we were waiting for. She informed me that someone would be along with a wheelchair soon since I was not able to walk.

I replied, "Oh, I believe I can. Let's go!" With a little help from my husband, I got out of bed and walked! (Remember, I'm not supposed to be able to walk!)

God is still in control!

So, after three days (rather than three weeks) in ICU, they moved me to my own room. I was so happy to be out of ICU. It was so cold in there, and the doctor would not let me get warm for fear of infection. They never turned the lights out and it was also very noisy, making it difficult to rest. Now I could rest without lights in my one eye that would not close.

Surgery Again

The days passed slowly in the hospital, but my progress was rapid. In fact, Dr. Schwartz asked me to go to another doctors' conference during this time. Only one week after surgery they took me down to the hospital auditorium again. The doctors were all amazed at my progress—I could walk, placing one foot directly in front of the other; I could close my eyes and touch my nose with the tip of my finger; and I could talk rationally. These may seem like small things, but most of their patients could not do this after brain surgery.

Two weeks after they removed the

tumor, I was back in surgery. This time it was for a nerve transplant. During the first surgery they had to cut the eighth nerve, which controls the left side of my face and my hearing. This transplant would only serve to help me close my eye and relax my face a little. It would never completely replace the one that was severed.

Rather than talking to me about this, the doctors discussed it with my husband. The procedure would involve getting a nerve from somewhere to use for the transplant, so they gave him two options: they could take the nerve out of my shoulder or out of my tongue.

Dr. Schwartz explained, "If we take the nerve out of her tongue, she will have to learn to talk again. Half of her tongue will atrophy, possibly leaving her with a permanent speech impediment. She will be able to close her left eye with a movement of her tongue. We know she has done everything we said she could not do, but this time will be different. She will not be able to speak for a while. If we take the nerve from her shoulder, the recovery of partial movement will take longer and she will have to move her shoulder in a certain way in order to close her eye."

My husband's choice was easy: "Take it out of her tongue!" (Sorry, honey, it did not work—I can still talk!)

They told him that I could learn to close my eye after this transplant by moving my tongue. The nerve does not realize it has been moved; it is still programmed to work with the tongue. So I have learned to control my left eye with my tongue.

They did not come for me until around two in the afternoon, making the surgery last past visiting hours. The hospital was very strict about visiting hours so my family was told they would have to go home. The nurse informed them the hospital would call if there was a problem; otherwise, they could come back in the morning and see me.

They actually cut my ear almost off and went through to my tongue and took a nerve. Then they transplanted the nerve behind my left ear and pointed it toward my spine. This nerve would grow a tiny bit, providing some movement and life, but it would never replace the nerve that had been severed.

This was another seven and one-half hour surgery. Before going into surgery this time I asked Dr. Schwartz to allow me to go back to my room rather than ICU if the surgery went well.

I was placed in recovery for a while and then sent to ICU. As they were wheeling me down the hall, I asked where they were taking me. When the nurse said ICU, I said "No, I don't belong in there." Of course she thought I did not know what I was talking about. (Remember, I am not supposed to even be able to talk at this time!)

When we stopped outside ICU the head nurse heard the commotion and came out to see what was going on. The nurse's aid wheeling me down told her, "She says she does not belong in here, but she just came out of seven and one-half hours of surgery."

The head nurse looked at my chart and barked, "She *doesn't* belong in here. Take her to her room!" In situations like this, one learns to be thankful for small favors.

The next morning a little before eight, I was sitting up in bed with all the tubes and IVs out, talking on the phone! This was only about eleven hours after surgery.

I had wanted to talk with Randy, our son, before he left for school. When my husband answered the phone and heard my voice he began to cry. I asked him what was wrong. (Was he crying because I could talk?) Then he told me what the doctor had told him: I was not supposed to be able to talk for a while, and then not without a speech impediment.

God is still in control!

Roffie at home after surgery wearing her wig. Underneath the hair is a bald head!

Home Again

Two weeks later I went home after four weeks in the hospital. This was just a few days before my twenty-eighth birthday. It was wonderful to be outside and to see the beautiful fall colors in St. Louis. Sister Bessie Pugh took us all to her house for a few days and cared for me in her kind way. Then Randy and I flew to Texas to spend a couple of weeks with Mother and Daddy and to get Debbie, while my husband attended the General Conference.

That was in October 1969. In November we moved from the apartment in St. Louis to a home in suburban Maryland

Heights. I was well enough to take part in the moving and even entertain company during the Christmas holidays.

Sometimes when we face a trying situation that leaves us handicapped, it is easy to concentrate on what we lost rather than on what we still have. I found that when I focused on what God preserved, it was easy to see how blessed I really was.

The doctors presumed that I would not be able to walk without staggering. They figured that I would shuffle, scoot, or waddle like a duck. They thought I would never be able to talk plainly. I was supposed to have to learn all the basics again. None of this happened!

However, I am without hearing in my left ear. Half of my tongue, part of my throat and the left side of my face is paralyzed. My tongue only operates on one side making it somewhat difficult to eat. My throat is dry on one side which makes it easy for me to choke.

Many people tried to convince me that

if I would just believe, God would completely heal me. I wrestled with this idea for several months and then I prayed through about it, reaching the point where I could say, "Lord, I trust Your judgment in this. If You choose to heal me, fine. If not, I will still serve and trust You."

A few years ago after giving my testimony at a ladies' retreat in Arizona, Sister Gwen Oakes stated that God had left His mark on me like He did on Jacob. This helped me realize that more people believe all this really happened when they see the residual effects of the surgery.

I have learned if I do not let it bother me, people do not even notice. Most of the time it is the little children that ask what is wrong with my face, embarrassing their parents. This has never bothered me. My family has laughed with me about the things I can do that they cannot do.

In 1991 I saw an article in our newspaper that stated, "Welcome to the '90s—the decade of fear!" I thought back to the time after surgery when it would have been easy to live in fear. Every headache could have triggered a new wave of fear, but I decided it was not God's will for His children to live in fear. God has not given us a spirit of fear (II Timothy 1:7).

I decided right up front that if God took care of me this time, He could do it again. He is the One who holds the keys to life and death. So, devil, I will not live in fear the rest of my life!

Please understand, dear reader, that God did not do this for me because of who I am but because of who He is. The faithfulness of God has nothing to do with who we are, but everything to do with who He is!

If we believe not, yet he abideth faithful: he cannot deny himself (II Timothy 2:13).

God is still God and He still has His way in the storm. Whatever He has done one time He can do again. He is the same yesterday, today and forever. He never changes!

> *Every good gift and every perfect gift is from above, and cometh down from the Father of lights, with whom is no variableness, neither shadow of turning* (James 1:17).

And remember this old song:

He'll do it again,
He'll do it again
Just take a look at where you are
now and where you have been
Hasn't He always come
through for you
He's the same now as then
You may not know how,
you may not know when,
But He'll do it again!

If you are in the midst of a storm today that is challenging your faith, I trust you will be strengthened and encouraged by this testimony of what God can do. May this help you to focus on the abundant supply of our God's riches rather than on the problem.

When Jesus came walking on the water to His disciples, the Bible tells us He would have passed them by if they had not called out to Him. The purpose for Him walking on the water was to show the disciples that what was troubling them was not a problem to Him. He saw them while He was still on the mountain and He could have calmed the storm before He came to them, but He chose not to.

We do not always understand why we go through the things we do, but the principle He taught His disciples that night is a good one to remember in a time of trouble: What is troubling us does not trouble Him. What may be threatening to inundate us is under His feet!

Epilogue

Reflecting on these events and the prayer I prayed over three decades ago, I am aware that God not only answered my prayer, but He did exceeding, abundantly above all that I could have imagined.

Now unto him that is able to do exceeding abundantly above all that we ask or think, according to the power that worketh in us (Ephesians 3:20).

In the past thirty-three years my husband and I have pastored in Texarkana, Arkansas; served as vice-president of Texas Bible College; pastored in Wichita Falls, Texas; and served as President of Texas Bible College for fourteen years. We are currently serving as associate pastor with our son at Living Way Church in Conroe, Texas. We also serve as the directors of ExCeLL, the extension ministry of Texas Bible College.

I have lived to see my children grow up, get married and have children. Now their children are having children, making us great-grandparents.

I have lived to experience things I would never have known had it not been for the mercy of a great and loving God.

I would never have known my "daughter-in-love" (she is that because my son loves her), Dovey Ensey. I would never have known my handsome grandsons—Brian, Michael, and Jonathan Ensey. I would never have known my grand-daughters-in-love, Stacey and Rebecca. I would never have known my great-grandson, Charles Alexander Ensey.

Brian and Stacey are Senior Bible Quizzing coaches and also teach the youth class, along with many other responsibilities. Michael and Rebecca serve as assistant pastor for Living Way Church. Jonathan plays the drums and keyboard, is our top senior quizzer, and is a leader among our young people.

I would never have known my "son-in-love" (he is that because my daughter loves him), Michael Black. I would never have known my lovely granddaughters, Lindsay and Lauren Black. Debbie and Mike pastor the First United Pentecostal Church in Statesville, North Carolina. Their daughters are both very involved in the church.

I would never have known hundreds of you wonderful people of God—hundreds of students that went through Texas Bible College, and hundreds more that I have taught in seminars and ladies' meetings in the past three decades.

My life has been enriched by knowing

each of you—my children, my children-in-love, my grandchildren, my great grandchildren, and a multitude of friends.

In these past thirty-three years I have been able to help my husband in almost every aspect of the ministry. We just celebrated forty-two years of marriage!

My prayer and desire today is still the same as it was that night so long ago: "Lord, when you get ready to take me, I want to be ready!"

Granddaughters Lindsay and Lauren with Lauren smiling like G'Ma

From A Husband's Perspective

I grew up on the plains of West Texas. Storms can come up there rather quickly. We discovered early in our marriage that storms can rapidly arise in our lives as well.

The news of Roffie's condition came so swiftly that we hardly had time to consider what was really happening. The symptoms had been there for some time, but a brain tumor? A fifty-fifty chance of surviving? Possibly a human vegetable? Walking like a duck and speaking with a slur? It was all incomprehensible. Yet reality has a way of alighting upon our tidy little lives at the most inopportune time.

One's world can become inverted overnight. Bad news causes all else to become secondary. That which seemed so imperative yesterday is not even on the agenda today.

It may seem easy to speak of the calm trust of one so close to you, but I have seen hundreds of life-threatening and terminal cases in nearly fifty years of ministry. None of those so afflicted has exceeded her in assurance, pure trust, and dogged determination to win over the adversity. And win she did. It left its slight mark on her but she sent it spinning through the ropes. Quitters never win and winners never quit. She was and is a winner.

She suffered the hand-wringers, the worry-warts, and the doomsayers with patience and kindness. They deterred her from full trust none at all. They meant well and she tolerated them, as well as those at the other extreme of the faith spectrum. She never claimed that she would be totally healed or be left without any sign of its passing. She did say that everything would be "okay." Faith is sometimes foolish, and within its bounds, that is a legitimate expression. There is often a fine line between faith and folly. But trust is more the "steady as she goes" attitude.

Trust was the attitude manifested by Shadrach, Meshach, and Abednego when their lives were threatened: "Our God whom we serve is able to deliver us from the burning fiery furnace...*but if not*, be it known unto thee, O king, we will not serve thy gods nor worship the golden image" (Daniel 3:17,18). They knew God *could* but were not positive that He *would* completely deliver them from death in the furnace. Some may criticize their faith as being the "could" variety rather than the "would" kind, but their absolute trust attracted the attention of the Lord.

Roffie's trust confounded the doctors from day one. She came through the surgery much better than they had dared to expect. She walked and talked when they said she couldn't. She got well faster, left the hospital sooner, and responded better than any patient they had seen in years—maybe ever. And who was surprised? No one who knew her well. Oh, that my faith had been at the level of hers. It was not. We all had confidence in God, but she shored up our trust with her indomitable spirit.

The last weekend before the surgery they sent her home to be with her family. We had such a wonderful time together. We tried not to think about all the possibilities, but they were always in the background. We all recognized that it could be our last weekend together. What mixed emotions we felt.

There were many ministers who came from all over the United States to pray for her and to be there with me during the surgery. I am thanking them yet again for their prayers and moral support. My entire family was there, many of Roffie's relatives were there, and our extended spiritual family from WEC and the St. Louis area filled the waiting rooms.

I was all tensed up during the seven and one-half hours of waiting. When the doctor sent word for me to come to where he was for a report, I could hardly breathe. I found Dr. Schwartz standing in the hallway near a nurses' station lighting his pipe. I suppose it was his way of unwinding after a long and arduous surgery. I hurriedly approached him and stood there without saying a word. Nor did he speak until he had taken a long pull at his pipe. As he exhaled, he said, "Well, she's alive." I was not overly shocked at that news—although he apparently thought that I should be—because I did not expect the worst in my heart of hearts.

But I said nothing, as I recall, just gave a sigh of relief. He was stressed from the lengthy and tedious surgery—seven and one-half hours with her brain exposed before him and when the slightest miscue would mean paralysis, a vegetative state, or even death. It must have been enormous pressure. Then he said, "But we did have to take the eighth nerve since the tumor had totally encapsulated it." I knew what he meant—partial paralysis of the face and neck. I flinched with disappointment and probably made some sound. Wrong thing! He lost his cool and began to berate me, calling me and my immediate relatives some very unflattering names. He figured I should be more thankful than that. I tried to find words to apologize for my insensitivity and he soon regathered his composure and finished his matter-of-fact report.

The first time I saw her after the surgery was quite traumatic. There she was—orange head, a small tuft of hair in the front sticking out from under the bandage, a clear plastic patch with gooey stuff in it over one eye, and her mouth seemed to be on the side of her face. But her spirit was intact. She was alert and ready to prove to every doctor and every nurse that she could do all the things that they said she couldn't. It was as if the whole ordeal made absolutely no difference to her.

The following weeks were long and lonely. The hospital was almost my home. When she was finally discharged, she went to the home of friends, and then when she was released to travel, she went to be with family in Texas.

She was sent home with a little machine that we used to give the side of her face an electric shock. Its purpose was to stimulate the muscles of the face so they did not atrophy before the transplanted nerve could take effect. We "shocked" her religiously for several weeks. Gradually the muscles and the new nerve took over and dissipated most of the appearance of paralysis.

The Lord spared her in order to continue her ministry as a wife, mother, helpmate, and as a speaker and teacher at women's conferences. She has given her testimony to many audiences, as large as thousands and as small as one. Many who have suffered a similar problem have called her for encouragement and solace. At providing that she has few peers.

So we see again how, through trust in God, a short-term negative situation was transformed into a long-term positive one. God has been doing that for six thousand years at least.

From Her Family's Perspective

Her Mother Remembers

As we waited in our home in Cleburne, Texas, for the results of the testing on our daughter, God was with us according to His word: "I will never leave you." I can't recall a moment of worry or even wondering why. I just knew that we were all in His hands, and what better place is there to be? We had taught our children to trust God in everything, do what you can and He will do what you can't. Now it was time for us to do just that.

When we got the news that it was a

brain tumor it was a shock because that had not come to mind. So each of us—David, 14, Gary, 12, my husband and I—went separately to a place of prayer. Later as we discussed how we prayed, we found that we had all prayed in one accord. We all knew that it was not a problem for God to heal, so we asked for healing, but each of us had also said, "Nevertheless, not my will but Thine be done."

We asked a friend, Mary, to come to our house and stay with our boys and Debbie, our four-year old granddaughter. This lady was not of the Pentecostal faith and she related the following story about Debbie when we got back home.

Mary said the first night Debbie had trouble going to sleep so she asked her if something was wrong. Debbie replied, "We didn't pray."

So Mary got up to pray with her and began to recite the Lord's Prayer. When she said, "Our Father," Debbie stopped praying. When Mary looked up, Debbie was standing there looking at her with her hands on her hips and said, "Mary, don't you even know His name?" Mary told me it was amazing for that little girl to be standing there teaching her something she did not know!

As we arrived in St. Louis, Brother Pugh picked us up at the airport. We asked how Roffie was and he replied, "Well, you would be surprised at Roffie. She said, 'Don't worry about me. I'll be all right.'"

My mind was saying, "No, I'm not surprised!"

We all cried the day we had to cut her beautiful long hair and have her head shaved. The doctors did not give us much hope and of course we hurt deeply for her, but through it all my heart was singing, "On Christ the solid Rock I stand!" Knowing we were all on the same page gave us assurance and hope. We were united in faith, and where there is unity there is strength.

After she was released from the hospital she wanted to come to Texas, but the doctors told her she would need therapy and could not be gone. She told them she could do her own therapy. She came to our house and brought her little machine that would make the muscles in her face work and used it while she was there. She would shock her face and then laugh at the way she looked. Laughter was probably as good for her as anything else. After all, the Bible tells us, "A merry heart doeth good like a medicine" (Proverbs 17:22).

    She sang while she was in the hospital and she is still singing thirty-three years later. She has done all the things the doctors said she would not do. Her attitude has been, "Who are they to tell me what I can and cannot do?"

Irene Oliver
Mother
at the age of 80

Her Sister Remembers

    I was only nine when Roffie married and left home. Some tall, handsome man came to our home and took her away. Not only did he take her away, he took her far away to places like Greensboro and St. Louis. Naturally, we did not get to see her and her growing family often but when she came home our household was filled with excitement and anticipation! Mother would begin cooking and preparing days in advance for their visit. Randy and Debbie, the youngest grandchildren, were growing up and we could barely sleep waiting for their arrival! Our younger brothers David and Gary were close in age to Randy and Debbie, and they looked forward to having someone their own age in the house. But more important, our big sister was coming home!

    As I got older I looked to Roffie to show me the latest hair styles and fashions. She made all her clothes and I thought she was the best-dressed lady around. Her hair came to the bend in her knees and was dark and curly. Just what I wanted but didn't get in the gene pool! My hair was blonde and straight. But she could always come up with a special style that would work well for my type of hair. After my engagement, Roffie began to help me plan my wedding and served as my matron of honor.

During this time she was experiencing severe, unexplained headaches. Occasionally she would fall and there seemed to be no reasonable explanation. None of our family had ever been ill for any length of time. Our family's religious heritage included a genuine trust and faith in the almighty God to be our source for every need. This meant physical, emotional, and spiritual needs. So when Roffie experienced headaches, we prayed for her healing and fully expected God to heal her. When the healing didn't come and other symptoms such as the unexplained falls came, we prayed more fervently. Once Roffie and I were in the car returning from a shopping trip (she was driving), when she temporarily lost her vision.

Now I must explain to you that Roffie is not one to complain. Her personality is very amiable and optimistic. So as the symptoms grew worse, we all knew that something was dreadfully wrong. Her illness was beginning to affect every aspect of her life.

After several attempts for medical help, Roffie still had no explanations for the headaches or falls. The next logical solution was to seek help for the unexplained and temporary loss of vision. During the exam, the optometrist commented that he was concerned that one of the veins to the eye did not seem to be delivering blood properly, indicating that there must be a blockage of some sort. He recommended that she see a well-known ophthalmologist for further testing. This testing led to the ultimate diagnosis of a brain tumor.

As I think back on this time, I can't remember one time thinking that Roffie would not make it through the surgery. My family never even discussed the possibility. We just continued to pray.

My husband, Bill, and I traveled with my parents to St. Louis to be with her and Jerry during the surgery. The doctors and nurses had somber faces as they explained each process to us. They needed to drill holes in her skull to place the appliance that would stabilize her head during the tedious surgery. Before they could take her for this procedure, her hair would have to be cut. Her hair had never been cut and as I cut the two braids of hair, her tears began to fall. I can remember all of us crying at the loss of her long, beautiful hair.

Surgery was scheduled for the following morning and much of the day was spent in preparation. The doctors and nurses tried to prepare us for the worst, but we continued to pray. I can remember thinking how sad that they didn't realize God could make everything all right. They told us that if Roffie lived, she might be no more than a vegetable. She perhaps would not be able to remember or recognize us. Her hearing was already partially impaired by the tumor. The piano she loved to play would be silent because she would not have the coordination to play or to even walk. God had to come to her rescue!

Surgery began early the next morning and the day seemed to be without end as we waited for a report. The chaplain of the hospital visited us and showed us the chapel where we could continue to pray. We would pray and we would meditate on the promises God had given us in His Word. I sat in the chapel and listened to my parents pray. Theirs were not elaborate or structured prayers. There was a desperate plea for mercy mixed with thanksgiving for what He and only He was able to do. They recognized that God doesn't make mistakes and whatever He chose to do would be the right choice. I listened to them encourage one another with the Scriptures. Our tears were for Roffie's suffering, not for fear that she would not make it.

Dr. Schwartz reported to us after more than seven hours of surgery that Roffie was alive, but warned us not to be too hopeful.

Later on we were limited to just a few minutes in the intensive care unit to see her. Never having witnessed anyone just out of brain surgery, I was shocked at how horrible she looked! Her head was bandaged and looked far too big for her body. I leaned over to kiss her cheek and called her name. Immediately she opened her eyes and called my name! Well, they were wrong on one count! She did know who I was and not only that, she could hear me! My faith began to soar! If the doctors were wrong on these things, then there was no telling what else she would be able to do!

The next days were just a whirlwind of excitement as day after day Roffie improved and baffled the medical community. Interns, residents, and medical doctors at the hospital visited her room to see for themselves the miraculous recovery.

After leaving the hospital, Roffie flew home to Texas to be reunited with her children and continue her recovery. Every day she improved. The sounds of her laughter and her music filled every room. There was no impaired coordination. There was no problem with her memory. God's Word had not failed us! His Word to us in Isaiah 53:5 was this: "But he was wounded for our transgressions, he was bruised for our iniquities; the chastisement of our peace was upon Him and with his stripes we are healed." All we had to do was believe and accept it. I expect that even though the doctors have seen miraculous healings, they have never forgotten the young lady from East Texas that never once wavered in her faith and what her God was able to do. Not one time had she lost that faith!

Recovery was a long process. There was the therapy and additional corrective surgery, but for Roffie there was no turning back. She was back in full swing and making up for lost time. Her hair was growing back and she and I together fixed wigs for her to wear.

June of the following year was camp meeting time in Lufkin and the four of us decided to pool our limited resources and attend. I'll never forget the laughter I heard coming from the bathroom as we were getting ready one evening. Roffie opened the door and called, "Gaye! Come watch me whistle!" Because of partial facial paralysis, she could only pucker half her mouth. We laughed together at how funny her mouth looked. I was too young at that time to realize just how incredible it was that she could actually laugh at her limitations.

As we have both grown older, I have developed a great respect and admiration for Roffie. She has never suffered any ill effects (such as depression) from this surgery. She has never once lamented about the loss of her facial muscles or the beautiful smile she had before the surgery. To me, she is still the most beautiful woman I know, inside and outside. She never wearies of helping others and is a great source of delight to all who know her. She enjoys life to its fullest.

I thank God for bringing Roffie through this "storm." There is no telling how this miraculous recovery has helped hundreds of others as they battled their own "storms." I give God all the glory and honor. I know it's made me stronger in my faith. Thank you, Roffie, for being a great role model to me and all who know you!

Gaye Cain
sister

Jerry and Roffie Ensey
2002

Randy and Dovey Ensey
2002
Pastor, Conroe, Texas

Brian, Stacey and Alexander Ensey
Michael and Rebecca Ensey
Jonathan Ensey
2002

Michael, Debbie, Lindsay and
Lauren Black
2002
Pastor, Statesville, NC

To **God** *Be The* **Glory!**
Great Things **HE** *Has Done!!*